Gallery Books
Editor: Peter Fallon

THE PARCHMENT BOAT

Moya Cannon

THE
PARCHMENT
BOAT

Gallery Books

The Parchment Boat
is first published
simultaneously in paperback
and in a clothbound edition
on 10 October 1997.

The Gallery Press
Loughcrew
Oldcastle
County Meath
Ireland

ISBN 1 85235 201 9 (*paperback*)
 1 85235 202 7 (*clothbound*)

The Gallery Press receives financial assistance from An Chomhairle
Ealaíon / The Arts Council, Ireland, and acknowledges also the assis-
tance of the Arts Council of Northern Ireland.

Contents

for Kathleen, Mary, Michael and John

*And so long as you haven't experienced
this: to die and so to grow,
you are only a troubled guest
on the dark earth.*

— Goethe,
*from 'The Holy Longing',
translated by Robert Bly*

Crannóg

Where an ash bush grows in the lake
a ring of stones has broken cover
in this summer's drought.
Not high enough to be an island,
it holds a disc of stiller water
in the riffled lake.

Trees have reclaimed the railway line behind us;
behind that, the road goes east —
as two lines parallel in space and time run away from us
this discovered circle draws us in.
In drowned towns
bells toll only for sailors and for the credulous
but this necklace of wet stones,
remnant of a wattle Atlantis,
catches us all by the throat.

We don't know what beads or blades
are held in the bog lake's wet amber
but much of us longs to live in water
and we recognise this surfacing
of old homes of love and hurt.

A troubled bit of us is kin
to people who drew a circle in water,
loaded boats with stone,
and raised a dry island and a fort
with a whole lake for a moat.

Shards

My garden is a graveyard for plates and cups
or else there's a bull in a china shop at the earth's core.
Each year's digging draws up a new hoard
and there's democracy in all the brokenness.
A blue pagoda lands next to a dandelion;
heavy delft and rosy wedding china
are beaten bright by the same May rain.
All equal now in the brown loam,
not all saw equal service or were mourned equally,
yet not one fragment gives anything away,
not a word of all they heard or saw,
or of the hands which used them roughly or with care —
dumb witnesses of hungers sated and thirsts slaked,
of the rare chances of communion,
before they were broken, and returned,
clay to clay,
having been through the fire
and having been a vessel for a while.

Introductions

Some of what we love
we stumble upon —
a purse of gold thrown on the road,
a poem, a friend, a great song.

And more
discloses itself to us —
a well among green hazels,
a nut thicket —
when we are worn out searching
for something quite different.

And more
comes to us, carried
as carefully
as a bright cup of water,
as new bread.

Murdering the Language

Why did I love
the neat examination of a noun under the pointer,
the analysis of a sentence lifted out of talk,
canal water halted in a lock?

> *Mood, tense, gender.*
> *What performs the action, what suffers the action?*
> *What governs what?*
> *What qualifies, modifies?*

When we whispered in our desks
we spoke our book of invasions —
an unruly wash of Victorian pedantry,
Cromwellian English, Scots,
the jetsam and the beached bones of Irish —
a grammarian's nightmare.

But we parsed a small rectangular sea
and never missed the flow
or wondered why victories won in blood are fastened in
    grammar
and in grammar's dream of order;
or why the dream of order draws us as surely as the dream
    of freedom
or why correct language is spoken only in the capital.

Our language was tidal;
it lipped the shale cliffs,
a long and tedious campaign,
and ran up the beaches, over sand, seaweed, stones.

Laws learned by heart in school are the hardest to unlearn,
but too much has been suffered since
in the name of who governs whom.
It is time to step outside the cold schools,
to find a new, less brutal grammar
which can allow what we know:
that this northern shore was wrought
not in one day, by one bright wave,
but by tholing the rush and tug of many tides.

Isolde's Tower, Essex Quay

It is our fictions which make us real.
— Robert Kroetch

Is there no end
to what can be dug up
out of the mud of a riverbank,

no end
to what can be dug up
out of the floodplains of a language?

This is no more
than the sunken stump
of a watchtower on a city wall,
built long after any Isolde might have lived,
built over since a dozen times,
uncovered now in some new work —
a tower's old root in black water
behind a Dublin bus stop;

and the story is no more than a story.
Tristan drifted in here on the tide to be healed,
taken in because of his music,
and a long yarn spun on
of which they'd say —

> *Had not the lovers of whom this story tells*
> *Endured sorrow for the sake of love*
> *They would never have comforted so many.*

Hunter's Moon

There are perhaps no accidents,
no coincidences.
When we stumble against people, books, rare moments
    out of time,
these are illuminations —
like the hunter's moon that sails tonight in its high clouds,
casting light into our black harbour,
where four black turf boats
tug at their ropes,
hunger for the islands.

Ontario Drumlin

Having run out the boat,
what stop of the heart
causes us to beach on the half-known
as Colmcille dragged up his skin boat
on the white strand of Iona?
An exile surely,
but the same salt-shriven grass,
the same wind at his heels.

Or what in me longs enough for the diminutive
in a continent of trees,
for this name to grip
here beside the Otonabee?
Druimlín,
little back, little hill,
a glacier kernel
rounded and stony
as any in Ulster's Cavan,
though the trees on it are red
and the hill's real name
is not heard.

Patched Kayak

(Royal Ontario Museum, Toronto)

Who made the parchment boat?
Who bent and bound ribs of drifted wood
to a long clean frame?
Who stretched sealskins,
plaited sinew,
stitched the stitches?
Which mapped the making,
which mapped the wounds,
which curved along the edges of the lives of seals,
the edges of the lives of women,
the edges of the lives of men.

Oysters

There is no knowing,
or hardly any,
more wondering —
for no one knows what joy the stone holds
in its stone heart,
or whether the lark is full of sorrow
as it springs against the sky.
What do we know, for instance,
of the ruminations of the oyster
which lies on the estuary bed —
not the rare, tormented pearl-maker,
just the ordinary oyster?
Does it dream away its years?

Or is it hard,
this existence where salt and river water mix?
The endless filtering
to sustain a pale silky life,
the labouring to build a grey shell,
incorporating all that floods and tides push in its way,
stones, mud, the broken shells of other fish.

Perhaps the oyster does not dream or think or feel at all
but then how can we understand
the pull of that huge muscle beside the heart
which clamps the rough shell shut
before a hunting starfish or a blade
but which opens it
to let in the tide?

Tending

When a wood fire burns down and falls apart
the fire in each log dies quickly
unless burnt ends are tilted together —
a moment's touch, recognition;
gold and blue flame
wraps the singing wood.

Viol

Wherever music comes from
it must come through an instrument.
Perhaps that is why we love the instrument best
which is most like us —

a long neck,
a throat that loves touch,
gut,
a body that resonates,

and life, the bow of hair and wood
which works us through the necessary cacophonous hours,
which welds dark and light into one deep tone,
which plays us, reluctant, into music.

Viola D'Amore

Sometimes love does die,
but sometimes, a stream on porous rock,
it slips down into the inner dark of a hill,
joins with other hidden streams
to travel blind as the white fish that live in it.
It forsakes one underground streambed
for the cave that runs under it.
Unseen, it informs the hill,
and, like the hidden strings of the *viola d'amore*,
makes the hill reverberate,
so that people who wander there
wonder why the hill sings,
wonder why they find wells.

Arctic Tern

Love has to take us unawares
for none of us would pay love's price if we knew it.
For who will pay to be destroyed?
The destruction is so certain,
so evident.

Much harder to chart,
less evident,
is love's second life,
a tern's egg,
revealed and hidden
in a nest of stones
on a stony shore.

What seems a stone
is no stone.
This vulnerable pulse
which could be held in the palm of a hand
may survive
to voyage the world's warm and frozen oceans,
its tapered wings,
the beat of its small heart,
a span between arctic poles.

Milk

Could he have known
that any stranger's baby
crying out loud in a street
can start the flow?
A stain that spreads
on fustian
or denim.

This is kindness
which in all our human time
has refused to learn propriety,
which still knows nothing
but the depth of kinship,
the depth of thirst.

Winter Paths

There is something about winter
which pares all living things down to their essentials —
a bare tree,
a black hedge,
hold their own stark thrones in our hearts.

Once, after searching a valley,
summer after summer,
I went in winter
and found at last the path
that linked the well to the little roofless churches —
a crooked way through fields.
Leafless, fruitless, the briar-bound stone walls
revealed their irregular gaps —
the way cattle and goats
and women and men
had passed, winter after winter,
drawing aside or shoving past stray strands of briar,
wondering if they'd know their way again in summer.

Hazelnuts

I thought that I knew what they meant
when they said that wisdom is a hazelnut.
You have to search the scrub
for hazel thickets,
gather the ripened nuts,
crack the hard shells,
and only then taste the sweetness at wisdom's kernel.

But perhaps it is simpler.
Perhaps it is we who wait in thickets
for fate to find us
and break us between its teeth
before we can start to know anything.

Mountain

Beauty can ambush us, even through a car window.
This green galleon sails eternally through Sligo,
dragging our hearts in its wake.

One singer was found by hunters on these green flanks
and another chose them as a deep cradle for his bones
but neither the Fianna's chroniclers nor Yeats
did more than pay their respects
to what was already here —

a mountain
which had already
shaken off glaciers,
carried a human cargo,
known grace in stone.

It might have been the same February light
on these tender slopes
which drew the first people from the coast
to set their fires on this plateau,
to build on this great limestone boat
whose boards are made of fishbones,
whose water is green time.

Scríob

Start again from nothing and scrape
since scraping is now part of us;
the sheep's track, the plough's track
are marked into the page,
the pen's scrape cuts a path on the hill.

But today I brought back
three bones of a bird,
eaten before it was hatched
and spat or shat out with its own broken shell
to weather on the north cliffs of Hoy.

This is an edge
where the pen runs dumb.
The small bleached bones of a fulmar or gannet
have nothing to tell.
They have known neither hunger nor flight
and have no understanding of the darkness
which came down and killed.

Tracks run to an end,
sheep get lost in the wet heather.
There are things which can neither be written, nor spoken,
        nor read;
thin wing bones which cannot be mended.

Too fragile for scraping,
the bones hold in their emptiness
the genesis of the first blown note.

Thole-Pin

Who speaks of victory? Endurance is all.

— Rainer Maria Rilke

Words, old tackle,
obsolete tools
moulder in outhouses, sheds of the mind —
the horse-collar rots on a high hook;
a flat-iron and an open razor rust together.

Sometimes a word is kept on
at just one task, its hardest,
in the corner of some trade or skill.
Thole survives,
a rough dowel
hammered into a boat's gunnel
to endure —
a pivot
seared between elements.

Easter Houses

During the last weeks of Lent
our play was earnest.
We'd hack sods out of the grass
and stack them among the trees
into four low walls.
The Easter house never had a roof —
what we needed was a place
where we could boil eggs outside.

After the battened-up heart of winter,
the long fast of spring,
life had come out again to nest in the open;
again, the shell was chipped open from within.

Song in Windsor, Ontario

Ice whispers
as it crushes against
steelbound, staggering timbers
in the Detroit river.

Great plates of ice from the lakes
catch on the banks,
turn under the March sun,
crumple each other
to show
how mountain ranges are made.

And on the wooden pylons,
a small bird
is back with the seed of music,
two notes,
the interval of desire
registered on the stirring cities.

Corrie

On the lake's lip
under this year's scribbles —
Phil and Fiona Feb 96 —
scores in red sandstone
show
where the glacier passed.

Having quarried out
the mountain's core,
it abandoned blocks of rock
at the valley's neck,
carried and scattered the rest
as it went down,
ground it into boulders,
red pebbles,
sand,

left behind
a bowl
of light.

Driving through Light in West Limerick

Poetry,
surpassing music, must take the place
of empty heaven and its hymns.
— Wallace Stevens

What's light that falls on nothing?
Nothing.
But this light turns wet trees into green lamps
and roadside grass into a green blaze
and lets the saffron hills run through our hearts
as though the world had no borders
and wet whin bushes were deeper than the sun.

What's light,
and who can hold it?
This morning, across the sea, in a gallery
I saw light held for five hundred years
on an angel's face —
a moment's surprise,
and centuries fell away
quiet as leaves.

But the angel's features
had been no more than any perfect features
until they'd caught the light
or else the light had fallen on them.

And trying to figure out
which had happened
I got off the Underground at King's Cross
and an accordion tune filled
the deep steel stairwell.

This was some descent of the strong sun,
good music
brought down to where it was needed,
music surpassing poetry
gone down again,
the busker with a red *Paolo Soprani*
telling again
of Orpheus in Connacht.

The escalators ground up and down
carrying all the people
up and down a hill
of saffron light.

Attention

Sometimes there is nothing,
absolutely nothing,
to be done but watch
and wait
and let the clock which breaks our days
let go its grasp
until the mind is able
to trust the storm
to bear up our weight of flesh and bone
to take on the time of breath
the rhythm of blood
a rhythm held
between two breaths
a bright cry
a last rasp.

Quartz

The roof of the well
is covered with chunks of white stone.
Among them lie an iron ring,
a six-inch iron nail made in a forge,
a cup with a blue flower.

This is the highest house on the shelf
because it has the highest well.

The woman who lived here,
at the end of a bad lane,
sat for the last few years
between fire and phone,
her quick eye on the window,
as a thirsty world kept coming
stepping in over small buckets of coal and kindling.

An Altered Gait

With the scurry of a sand-piper
a gull runs and runs along the tideline.
It trails something dark behind it,
the broken rim
of its right wing.

A fortnight ago
as my father lay dying
he sometimes lifted his good right arm,
the same troubled eye —
the same hurry told in his breath
as we waited
and he laboured
towards the flight out.

Bulbs

I put them down late, in November,
into the grass of the cold garden.
It is hard to believe that they will grow at all
or that the brown papery onions,
now stowed in the ground,
have life in them.

Yet before the frosts are finished
they will come up,
green spears through the grass,
like sleeping legions returning in our time of need.

That time is spring,
when courage is necessary and scarce,
when each green blade will break and yield up
last summer's hoarded sun.

Night

Coming back from Cloghane
in the sudden frost
of a November night,
I was ambushed
by the river of stars.

Disarmed by lit skies
I had utterly forgotten
this arc of darkness,
this black night
where the frost-hammered stars
were notes thrown from a chanter,
crans of light.

So I wasn't ready
for the dreadful glamour of Orion
as he struck out over Barr dTrí gCom
in his belt of stars.

At Gleann na nGealt
his bow of stars
was drawn against my heart.

What could I do?

Rather than drive into a pitch-black ditch
I got out twice,
leaned back against the car
and stared up at our windy, untidy loft

where old people had flung up old junk
they'd thought might come in handy,
ploughs, ladles, bears, lions, a clatter of heroes,
a few heroines, a path for the white cow, a swan
and, low down, almost within reach,
Venus, completely unfazed by the frost.

Migrations

The strong geese claim the sky again
and tell and tell and tell us
of the many shifts and weathers
of the long-boned earth.

Blind to their huge, water-carved charts,
our blood dull to the tug of poles,
we are tuned still to the rising and dying of light
and we still share their need
to nest and to journey.

Between the Jigs and the Reels

Between a jig and a reel
what is there?
Only one beat
escaped from a ribcage.

Tunes are migratory
and fly from heart to heart
intimating
that there's a pattern
to life's pulls and draws.

Because what matters to us most
can seldom be told in words
the heart's moods are better charted
in its own language —

the rhythm of Cooley's accordion
which could open the heart of a stone,
John Doherty's dark reels
and the tune that the sea taught him,
the high parts of the road and the underworlds
which only music and love can brave
to bring us back to our senses
and on beyond.

Author's Acknowledgements

I wish to acknowledge the assistance of An Chomhairle Ealaíon/The Arts Council, Ireland; Canada Council; Kerry County Council; Trent University, Ontario; The Verbal Arts Centre, Derry; and Waterford Corporation for their help in the time of the writing of these poems.